MAD LIBS®

SLEEPOVER PARTY
MAD LIBS

By Roger Price and Leonard Stern

Mad Libs
An Imprint of Penguin Random House

MAD LIBS
Penguin Young Readers Group
An Imprint of Penguin Random House LLC

Concept created by Roger Price & Leonard Stern

Published by Mad Libs,
an imprint of Penguin Random House LLC,
345 Hudson Street, New York, New York 10014.
Printed in the USA.

ISBN 9780843126990
45

MAD LIBS
INSTRUCTIONS

MAD LIBS® is a game for people who don't like games!
It can be played by one, two, three, four, or forty.

• RIDICULOUSLY SIMPLE DIRECTIONS

In this tablet you will find stories containing blank spaces where words
are left out. One player, the READER, selects one of these stories. The
READER does not tell anyone what the story is about. Instead, he/she asks
the other players, the WRITERS, to give him/her words. These words are
used to fill in the blank spaces in the story.

• TO PLAY

The READER asks each WRITER in turn to call out a word—an adjective or
a noun or whatever the space calls for—and uses them to fill in the blank
spaces in the story. The result is a MAD LIBS® game.

When the READER then reads the completed MAD LIBS® game to the other
players, they will discover that they have written a story that is fantastic,
screamingly funny, shocking, silly, crazy, or just plain dumb—depending
upon which words each WRITER called out.

• EXAMPLE (*Before* and *After*)

"_____!" he said _____
      EXCLAMATION   ADVERB

as he jumped into his convertible _____ and
                                              NOUN

drove off with his _____ wife.
                          ADJECTIVE

"____*Ouch*____!" he said ____*Stupidly*____
      EXCLAMATION   ADVERB

as he jumped into his convertible ____*cat*____ and
                                            NOUN

drove off with his ____*brave*____ wife.
                          ADJECTIVE

MAD LIBS®
QUICK REVIEW

In case you have forgotten what adjectives, adverbs, nouns, and verbs are, here is a quick review:

An ADJECTIVE describes something or somebody. Lumpy, soft, ugly, messy, and short are adjectives.

An ADVERB tells how something is done. It modifies a verb and usually ends in "ly." Modestly, stupidly, greedily, and carefully are adverbs.

A NOUN is the name of a person, place, or thing. Sidewalk, umbrella, bridle, bathtub, and nose are nouns.

A VERB is an action word. Run, pitch, jump, and swim are verbs. Put the verbs in past tense if the directions say PAST TENSE. Ran, pitched, jumped, and swam are verbs in the past tense.

When we ask for A PLACE, we mean any sort of place: a country or city (Spain, Cleveland) or a room (bathroom, kitchen).

An EXCLAMATION or SILLY WORD is any sort of funny sound, gasp, grunt, or outcry, like Wow!, Ouch!, Whomp!, Ick!, and Gadzooks!

When we ask for specific words, like a NUMBER, a COLOR, an ANIMAL, or a PART OF THE BODY, we mean a word that is one of those things, like seven, blue, horse, or head.

When we ask for a PLURAL, it means more than one. For example, cat pluralized is cats.

MAD LIBS® is fun to play with friends, but you can also play it by yourself! To begin with, DO NOT look at the story on the page below. Fill in the blanks on this page with the words called for. Then, using the words you have selected, fill in the blank spaces in the story.

Now you've created your own hilarious MAD LIBS® game!

YOU'RE INVITED

PERSON IN ROOM (FEMALE) _Exemo Kaitlyn_

ADJECTIVE _fun_

NOUN _internal organs_

NOUN _floor_

CELEBRITY _the Rock_

ADVERB _sadly_

NUMBER _31_

ADJECTIVE _juicy_

NOUN _forest_

NOUN _dogs_

PART OF THE BODY _celvic mustles_

PLURAL NOUN _balloons_

ADJECTIVE _fast_

PLURAL NOUN _houses_

PLURAL NOUN _spaghettis_

ADJECTIVE _hangry_

PLURAL NOUN _cars_

LETTER OF THE ALPHABET _n_

CELEBRITY _Alan walker_

SAME CELEBRITY _Alan walker_

ADJECTIVE _sad_

It's a sleepover!

MAD LIBS®
YOU'RE INVITED

Dear __Exemo kaitlyn__
PERSON IN ROOM (FEMALE)

I would like to invite you to a/an __ran__ sleepover
ADJECTIVE

party this Friday night at my __internal organs__. I live on the
NOUN

corner of South __Floor__ Street and __The Rock__
NOUN   CELEBRITY

Lane. Please arrive __sadly__ at __31__
ADVERB   NUMBER

o'clock. Don't forget to bring a/an __juicy__
ADJECTIVE

sleeping __forest__ and a soft __dog__ to rest your
NOUN   NOUN

__celvic muscles__ on. We'll have pizza topped with __balloons__
PART OF THE BODY   PLURAL NOUN

for dinner, and we'll watch a/an __fast__ movie. When
ADJECTIVE

it is time for bed, we'll all change into our __houses__ and
PLURAL NOUN

turn out the __spaghetties__. Then we'll tell __hangry__
PLURAL NOUN   ADJECTIVE

ghost stories and talk about all the cute __cars__
PLURAL NOUN

at school! Please RSV-__n__ to me by e-mail at
LETTER OF THE ALPHABET

iluv-__Alanwalker__ @ __alan walker__.com. Hope you
CELEBRITY   SAME CELEBRITY

can join our __sad__ party!
ADJECTIVE

MAD LIBS® is fun to play with friends, but you can also play it by yourself! To begin with, DO NOT look at the story on the page below. Fill in the blanks on this page with the words called for. Then, using the words you have selected, fill in the blank spaces in the story.

Now you've created your own hilarious MAD LIBS® game!

LET'S GET PACKING!

NOUN _lampost_

ADJECTIVE _lightly_

NOUN _Frech Fried Frog legs_

ADJECTIVE _Slimy_

PLURAL NOUN _bats_

NOUN _sky skraper_

PART OF THE BODY (PLURAL) _butt_

VERB _hop_

ADJECTIVE _delicius_

CELEBRITY _the Arock_

VERB _skip_

ADVERB _hungerly_

ADJECTIVE _breadenly_

NOUN _boble head_

VERB _breathi_

VERB ENDING IN "ING" _eating_

NOUN _Mars_

ADJECTIVE _small_

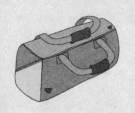

MAD LIBS®

LET'S GET PACKING!

If you are going to a sleepover at a friend's __lamp post__, here's

a/an __lightly__ list of things to put in your overnight
ADJECTIVE

__Frech Fried Frog legs__
NOUN

1. __slimy__ pajamas and a change of __bats__
   ADJECTIVE   PLURAL NOUN

   for the next day.

2. A tooth-__Sky skraper__ for brushing your __butt__.
   NOUN   PART OF THE BODY (PLURAL)

3. Some CDs so you and your friends can __hop__
   VERB

   to your favorite __delicus__ tunes.
   ADJECTIVE

4. Magazines with someone like __the rock__ on
   CELEBRITY

   the cover and articles about how to __skip__
   VERB

   __hungerly__.
   ADVERB

5. A/an __beathing__ __boble head__-light will help
   ADJECTIVE   NOUN

   you to __breathing__ in the dark while you stay up
   VERB

   __eating__ into the wee hours of the __Mars__.
   VERB ENDING IN "ING"   NOUN

If you follow this checklist, you should have a really __small__
ADJECTIVE

sleepover.

MAD LIBS® is fun to play with friends, but you can also play it by yourself! To begin with, DO NOT look at the story on the page below. Fill in the blanks on this page with the words called for. Then, using the words you have selected, fill in the blank spaces in the story.

Now you've created your own hilarious MAD LIBS® game!

PILLOW FIGHT!

ADJECTIVE _____

PERSON IN ROOM (FEMALE) _____

ADJECTIVE _____

NOUN _____

PART OF THE BODY _____

NOUN _____

PERSON IN ROOM (FEMALE) _____

PART OF THE BODY (PLURAL) _____

NOUN _____

PLURAL NOUN _____

ADJECTIVE _____

ADJECTIVE _____

ADJECTIVE _____

MAD☺LIBS®
PILLOW FIGHT!

The last time I went to a sleepover, a/an ___Spicy___ pillow
<u>ADJECTIVE</u>

fight broke out. Out of nowhere, ___Emma___ grabbed her
<u>PERSON IN ROOM (FEMALE)</u>

___delicious___, fluffy ___Brendon___ and began
<u>ADJECTIVE</u>   <u>NOUN</u>

swinging it at anyone close to her. Soon, everyone else joined in!

At one point, I got hit right in the back of my ___toes___.
<u>PART OF THE BODY</u>

As soon as I recovered, I tossed my ___crayon___ at
<u>NOUN</u>

___Rebecca___'s ___feet___, but I missed. Instead,
<u>PERSON IN ROOM (FEMALE)</u>   <u>PART OF THE BODY (PLURAL)</u>

I knocked over an expensive ___Kaitlyn___ and my pillow
<u>NOUN</u>

split open! ___Broden's___ flew everywhere, covering the
<u>PLURAL NOUN</u>

room in a layer of ___Brendonde___ feathers. The fighting
<u>ADJECTIVE</u>

stopped when we all broke out in ___tasty___ laughter.
<u>ADJECTIVE</u>

The fun ended when we realized we had to clean up the

___bloody___ mess!
<u>ADJECTIVE</u>

MAD LIBS® is fun to play with friends, but you can also play it by yourself! To begin with, DO NOT look at the story on the page below. Fill in the blanks on this page with the words called for. Then, using the words you have selected, fill in the blank spaces in the story.

Now you've created your own hilarious MAD LIBS® game!

SLEEPWALKING

VERB ENDING IN "ING" _____

ADJECTIVE _____

PLURAL NOUN _____

PLURAL NOUN _____

VERB _____

PART OF THE BODY (PLURAL) _____

VERB _____

ADJECTIVE _____

NOUN _____

NOUN _____

PLURAL NOUN _____

ADJECTIVE _____

NOUN _____

SILLY WORD _____

PLURAL NOUN _____

MAD☺LIBS®
SLEEPWALKING

Sleep-___fishing___ is a/an ___lively___ phenomenon
<small>VERB ENDING IN "ING"</small>　　　　　　<small>ADJECTIVE</small>

that a surprising number of ___organs___ experience.
<small>PLURAL NOUN</small>

Usually, sleepwalkers climb out of their ___interiors___ and
<small>PLURAL NOUN</small>

begin to ___dying___ with their ___stomachs___
<small>VERB</small>　　　　　　<small>PART OF THE BODY (PLURAL)</small>

tightly shut. Sometimes they ___running___ outdoors
<small>VERB</small>

wearing only their ___unbearable___ pajamas. And it's not
<small>ADJECTIVE</small>

uncommon for ___pop-tart___ -walkers to raid the
<small>NOUN</small>

___Emma___ and eat lots of ___pencils___.
<small>NOUN</small>　　　　　　<small>PLURAL NOUN</small>

What's truly amazing is that they don't remember a/an

___gross___ thing the following ___Rebecca___.
<small>ADJECTIVE</small>　　　　　　<small>NOUN</small>

They'll open the fridge and say, "___bagibajaba___! Where did
<small>SILLY WORD</small>

all the ___flies___ go?" They may never know!
<small>PLURAL NOUN</small>

MAD LIBS® is fun to play with friends, but you can also play it by yourself! To begin with, DO NOT look at the story on the page below. Fill in the blanks on this page with the words called for. Then, using the words you have selected, fill in the blank spaces in the story.

Now you've created your own hilarious MAD LIBS® game!

M.A.S.H.

ADJECTIVE _____

NUMBER _____

PLURAL NOUN _____

A PLACE _____

PERSON IN ROOM (MALE) _____

ADJECTIVE _____

A PLACE _____

ADJECTIVE _____

ADJECTIVE _____

NOUN _____

A PLACE _____

ADJECTIVE _____

NUMBER _____

NOUN _____

NUMBER _____

OCCUPATION _____

NOUN _____

ADJECTIVE _____

MAD LIBS®
M.A.S.H.

Congratulations! According to M.A.S.H. (the ultimate sleepover

game), your future looks bright and _____. When you
                                         ADJECTIVE

are _____ years old, you will meet the man of your
          NUMBER

_____ at (the) _____. His name will be
   PLURAL NOUN   A PLACE

_____. You will have a/an _____
PERSON IN ROOM (MALE)   ADJECTIVE

wedding, and you will go to (the) _____ on your
                                        A PLACE

_____ honeymoon. When you return, you will move
   ADJECTIVE

into a/an _____ _____ in (the)
                 ADJECTIVE   NOUN

_____. You will drive a/an _____ car. Then,
     A PLACE   ADJECTIVE

when you have been married for _____ years, you
                                      NUMBER

will have your first _____. You will go on to have
                            NOUN

_____ more children. You will work as a/an _____
   NUMBER   OCCUPATION

until you retire and move to a tropical _____.
                                               NOUN

Your M.A.S.H. future looks prosperous and _____, so
                                                 ADJECTIVE

prepare to enjoy it!

From SLEEPOVER PARTY MAD LIBS® • Copyright © 2008 by Penguin Random House LLC.

MAD LIBS® is fun to play with friends, but you can also play it by yourself! To begin with, DO NOT look at the story on the page below. Fill in the blanks on this page with the words called for. Then, using the words you have selected, fill in the blank spaces in the story.

Now you've created your own hilarious MAD LIBS® game!

PRANKS FOR NOTHING

ADJECTIVE _____

ADJECTIVE _____

PLURAL NOUN _____

ADJECTIVE _____

PLURAL NOUN _____

PLURAL NOUN _____

ADJECTIVE _____

VERB ENDING IN "ING" _____

NOUN _____

NOUN _____

ADJECTIVE _____

NOUN _____

ADJECTIVE _____

PART OF THE BODY _____

ADJECTIVE _____

PLURAL NOUN _____

PART OF THE BODY (PLURAL) _____

ADJECTIVE _____

PART OF THE BODY (PLURAL) _____

COLOR _____

MAD LIBS®
PRANKS FOR NOTHING

Whenever my _____ sister and her _____
                ADJECTIVE   ADJECTIVE

_____ have a sleepover party, I love to play
   PLURAL NOUN

_____ pranks on them. Once, I put gummy
   ADJECTIVE

_____ in everyone's sleeping _____.
   PLURAL NOUN   PLURAL NOUN

They thought they were _____ bugs, and they were
                              ADJECTIVE

out of their _____ bags in record time! Another
          VERB ENDING IN "ING"

time, I hid all the rolls of _____ paper in the
                         NOUN

trunk of Dad's _____, not knowing that Dad, a/an
                NOUN

_____ doctor, was on duty at the _____
   ADJECTIVE   NOUN

that night. But the most _____ prank of all time
                         ADJECTIVE

was when I replaced all of the _____-paste with
                          PART OF THE BODY

_____ icing. When my sister's _____
   ADJECTIVE   PLURAL NOUN

brushed their _____ with it, the _____
        PART OF THE BODY (PLURAL)   ADJECTIVE

looks on their _____ were priceless—but the
        PART OF THE BODY (PLURAL)

_____ icing all over their teeth was even better!
   COLOR

MAD LIBS® is fun to play with friends, but you can also play it by yourself! To begin with, DO NOT look at the story on the page below. Fill in the blanks on this page with the words called for. Then, using the words you have selected, fill in the blank spaces in the story.

Now you've created your own hilarious MAD LIBS® game!

LIGHT AS A FEATHER

ADJECTIVE _____

ADJECTIVE _____

ADJECTIVE _____

ADJECTIVE _____

NOUN _____

PLURAL NOUN _____

PART OF THE BODY (PLURAL) _____

ADVERB _____

ADJECTIVE _____

NUMBER _____

NOUN _____

NOUN _____

NOUN _____

ADVERB _____

NOUN _____

NOUN _____

ADVERB _____

PLURAL NOUN _____

ADJECTIVE _____

MAD☺LIBS®
LIGHT AS A FEATHER

Another _____ sleepover game is _____
              ADJECTIVE   ADJECTIVE

as a feather, _____ as a board. You'll need a/an
                    ADJECTIVE

_____ volunteer to lie down on the _____
    ADJECTIVE   NOUN

with her _____ closed and her _____
              PLURAL NOUN   PART OF THE BODY (PLURAL)

folded across her chest. Tell her to breathe _____ and
                                                      ADVERB

remain _____ and relaxed. Then gather in a circle around
              ADJECTIVE

her, placing _____ fingers underneath her _____
                  NUMBER   NOUN

as you repeat the phrase, "Light as a/an _____, stiff as
                                                  NOUN

a/an _____." On the count of three, _____ lift
          NOUN   ADVERB

her off the _____ and raise her to the _____.
                NOUN   NOUN

Then lower her down _____. Your _____
                          ADVERB   PLURAL NOUN

will be completely amazed at this _____ feat!
                                        ADJECTIVE

MAD LIBS® is fun to play with friends, but you can also play it by yourself! To begin with, DO NOT look at the story on the page below. Fill in the blanks on this page with the words called for. Then, using the words you have selected, fill in the blank spaces in the story.

Now you've created your own hilarious MAD LIBS® game!

LET'S DANCE!

ADJECTIVE _____

PLURAL NOUN _____

NUMBER _____

PLURAL NOUN _____

ADJECTIVE _____

ADVERB _____

ADJECTIVE _____

NOUN _____

VERB (PAST TENSE) _____

PART OF THE BODY _____

PERSON IN ROOM _____

ADJECTIVE _____

NUMBER _____

PART OF THE BODY _____

ADVERB _____

ADJECTIVE _____

PLURAL NOUN _____

ADVERB _____

PLURAL NOUN _____

NOUN _____

PART OF THE BODY (PLURAL) _____

MAD LIBS®
LET'S DANCE!

At my _____ sleepover party, my best _____
       ADJECTIVE   PLURAL NOUN

and I decided to have a dance-off. We made my _____-
                                                NUMBER

year-old little sister be the judge. We broke into two teams, "The

_____" and "The _____ Dancers." My team
PLURAL NOUN   ADJECTIVE

danced _____, but the other team's _____
          ADVERB   ADJECTIVE

moves were out of this _____! They totally out-
                      NOUN

_____ us. So when no one was looking, I grabbed my
VERB (PAST TENSE)

sister by the _____ and pulled her aside. "_____,"
        PART OF THE BODY   PERSON IN ROOM

I whispered, "I promise to do all of your _____ chores
                                  ADJECTIVE

for _____ months if you say that my team won." My sister
    NUMBER

shook her _____. "No way!" she said _____.
      PART OF THE BODY   ADVERB

"Your team danced worse than a bunch of _____
                                ADJECTIVE

_____!" "Fine," I said. "Then I'll just have to tell all of
PLURAL NOUN

my friends that you're _____ afraid of _____."
                  ADVERB   PLURAL NOUN

That helped to change her _____. We won that
                            NOUN

contest, _____ down!
   PART OF THE BODY (PLURAL)

MAD LIBS® is fun to play with friends, but you can also play it by yourself! To begin with, DO NOT look at the story on the page below. Fill in the blanks on this page with the words called for. Then, using the words you have selected, fill in the blank spaces in the story.

Now you've created your own hilarious MAD LIBS® game!

SNORE NO MORE

ADJECTIVE _____

NOUN _____

NOUN _____

ADJECTIVE _____

VERB ENDING IN "ING" _____

VERB _____

PART OF THE BODY _____

VERB ENDING IN "ING" _____

ADJECTIVE _____

ADJECTIVE _____

ADJECTIVE _____

VERB ENDING IN "ING" _____

ADJECTIVE _____

ADJECTIVE _____

PART OF THE BODY _____

MAD LIBS®

SNORE NO MORE

Snoring is a loud and often _____ sound that can be
                            ADJECTIVE

compared to sawing a piece of _____ or to a freight
                               NOUN

_____ roaring down the tracks. Fortunately, there are many
NOUN

_____ solutions to keep a snorer from _____:
ADJECTIVE   VERB ENDING IN "ING"

1. _____ on your _____ instead of on
        VERB   PART OF THE BODY

   your back.

2. Try _____ without a/an _____ pillow.
       VERB ENDING IN "ING"   ADJECTIVE

3. Learn to play the didgeridoo, a/an _____
                                         ADJECTIVE

   Australian wind instrument. Studies have shown that this

   strengthens _____ airways and helps reduce
                   ADJECTIVE

   _____. The trouble with this _____
   VERB ENDING IN "ING"   ADJECTIVE

   solution is that most people can't stand the _____
                                                    ADJECTIVE

   sound of the didgeridoo.

4. If all else fails and the snoring continues, buy a pair of

   _____-plugs for anyone sleeping nearby!
   PART OF THE BODY

MAD LIBS® is fun to play with friends, but you can also play it by yourself! To begin with, DO NOT look at the story on the page below. Fill in the blanks on this page with the words called for. Then, using the words you have selected, fill in the blank spaces in the story.

Now you've created your own hilarious MAD LIBS® game!

PIZZA PARTY

CELEBRITY _____

ADJECTIVE _____

NUMBER _____

ADJECTIVE _____

PLURAL NOUN _____

PLURAL NOUN _____

NOUN _____

ADJECTIVE _____

PLURAL NOUN _____

PLURAL NOUN _____

ADJECTIVE _____

PLURAL NOUN _____

PLURAL NOUN _____

NOUN _____

MAD LIBS®
PIZZA PARTY

CLERK: Hello, _____'s Pizza Shop. How can I help you?
　　　　　　　　　　　CELEBRITY

GIRL: I'm having a/an _____ party, and I would like
　　　　　　　　　　　　　ADJECTIVE

to order enough pizza for _____ _____
　　　　　　　　　　　　　　　　NUMBER　　　　　　　ADJECTIVE

people.

CLERK: Five large _____ should be enough. What
　　　　　　　　　　　PLURAL NOUN

_____ would you like on them? Tonight's special is
　　PLURAL NOUN

pizza topped with _____ cheese, _____
　　　　　　　　　　　　NOUN　　　　　　　　　　　ADJECTIVE

tomatoes, and green _____.
　　　　　　　　　　　　PLURAL NOUN

GIRL: Can you add sliced _____ and _____
　　　　　　　　　　　　　　PLURAL NOUN　　　　　　　　ADJECTIVE

onions, too?

CLERK: Can do. Since you're ordering more than fifty _____-
　　　　　　　　　　　　　　　　　　　　　　　　　　PLURAL NOUN

worth of food, you get free _____ for dessert.
　　　　　　　　　　　　　　　PLURAL NOUN

GIRL: Thanks. And please hurry. We're so hungry, we could eat a/an

_____!
　　NOUN

MAD LIBS® is fun to play with friends, but you can also play it by yourself! To begin with, DO NOT look at the story on the page below. Fill in the blanks on this page with the words called for. Then, using the words you have selected, fill in the blank spaces in the story.

Now you've created your own hilarious MAD LIBS® game!

NO BOYS ALLOWED!

PERSON IN ROOM (MALE) _____

ADJECTIVE _____

NOUN _____

PLURAL NOUN _____

ADJECTIVE _____

ADJECTIVE _____

ADJECTIVE _____

PART OF THE BODY _____

PLURAL NOUN _____

PART OF THE BODY (PLURAL) _____

PLURAL NOUN _____

MAD LIBS®
NO BOYS ALLOWED!

Attention, _____! _____ boys are NOT
          PERSON IN ROOM (MALE)   ADJECTIVE

allowed to enter this room. This ESPECIALLY goes for _____-
                                                         NOUN

faced brothers like you! There is a/an _____-only
                                            PLURAL NOUN

_____ party in progress, and you are not invited. If
      ADJECTIVE

you dare enter, be aware that you are a target for _____
                                                        ADJECTIVE

pranks. We may even subject you to a/an _____
                                             ADJECTIVE

makeover and put makeup on your _____ before
                                      PART OF THE BODY

we let you escape. So, if you are made of _____ and
                                                PLURAL NOUN

snails and puppy-dog _____, please go back to
                      PART OF THE BODY (PLURAL)

where you came from. No _____ allowed!
                             PLURAL NOUN

MAD LIBS® is fun to play with friends, but you can also play it by yourself! To begin with, DO NOT look at the story on the page below. Fill in the blanks on this page with the words called for. Then, using the words you have selected, fill in the blank spaces in the story.

Now you've created your own hilarious MAD LIBS® game!

MIDNIGHT MOVIES

ADJECTIVE _____

ADJECTIVE _____

PERSON IN ROOM (FEMALE) _____

NOUN _____

ADJECTIVE _____

NOUN _____

PLURAL NOUN _____

ADJECTIVE _____

ADJECTIVE _____

NOUN _____

NOUN _____

PART OF THE BODY _____

PLURAL NOUN _____

PERSON IN ROOM (FEMALE) _____

NOUN _____

NOUN _____

ADJECTIVE _____

NOUN _____

MAD☻LIBS®

MIDNIGHT MOVIES

Looking for the perfect movie to watch at your sleepover? Try one

of these _____ party favorites:
       _____ADJECTIVE_____

- _____ *Girls:* This film stars _____
  _____ADJECTIVE_____   PERSON IN ROOM (FEMALE)

  Lohan as a homeschooled _____ who goes to
                              _____NOUN_____

  a/an _____ high school for the first time. Will
        _____ADJECTIVE_____

  she turn into a mean _____ like the rest of the
                          _____NOUN_____

  popular _____?
           _____PLURAL NOUN_____

- *Legally* _____: In this movie, a/an _____
          _____ADJECTIVE_____   _____ADJECTIVE_____

  sorority _____ follows her ex-boyfriend to an
            _____NOUN_____

  Ivy _____ school in an attempt to win back his
       _____NOUN_____

  _____.
  _____PART OF THE BODY_____

- *The Princess* _____: When _____
                 _____PLURAL NOUN_____   PERSON IN ROOM (FEMALE)

  Thermopolis discovers she is a/an _____ and
                                     _____NOUN_____

  an heir to the _____ of a/an _____
                  _____NOUN_____   _____ADJECTIVE_____

  country, her entire _____ is turned upside down.
                       _____NOUN_____

MAD LIBS® is fun to play with friends, but you can also play it by yourself! To begin with, DO NOT look at the story on the page below. Fill in the blanks on this page with the words called for. Then, using the words you have selected, fill in the blank spaces in the story.

Now you've created your own hilarious MAD LIBS® game!

A GHASTLY GHOST STORY
(PART 1)

ADJECTIVE _____

PLURAL NOUN _____

NOUN _____

NOUN _____

ADJECTIVE _____

PLURAL NOUN _____

NOUN _____

VERB (PAST TENSE) _____

ADJECTIVE _____

NOUN _____

ADJECTIVE _____

PART OF THE BODY (PLURAL) _____

MAD LIBS®
A GHASTLY GHOST STORY
(PART 1)

One dark and _____ night I had a sleepover party with
             ADJECTIVE

seven _____ at my family's old Victorian _____
   PLURAL NOUN   NOUN

at the edge of town. I was the first person in the house to fall asleep,

and in the middle of the _____, I was startled awake by a/an
                     NOUN

_____ sound coming from the attic. I couldn't stop my
 ADJECTIVE

_____ from shaking as I slipped into a/an _____,
 PLURAL NOUN   NOUN

_____ upstairs, and opened the door to the attic. Out of
VERB (PAST TENSE)

nowhere, a/an _____ figure in a pale white _____
            ADJECTIVE   NOUN

with long _____ hair flew past me. Terrified, I screamed at
        ADJECTIVE

the top of my _____.
      PART OF THE BODY (PLURAL)

MAD LIBS® is fun to play with friends, but you can also play it by yourself! To begin with, DO NOT look at the story on the page below. Fill in the blanks on this page with the words called for. Then, using the words you have selected, fill in the blank spaces in the story.

Now you've created your own hilarious MAD LIBS® game!

A GHASTLY GHOST STORY (PART 2)

NOUN _____

VERB ENDING IN "ING" _____

NOUN _____

PLURAL NOUN _____

NOUN _____

PART OF THE BODY _____

PLURAL NOUN _____

PLURAL NOUN _____

ADJECTIVE _____

ADJECTIVE _____

ADVERB _____

NOUN _____

NOUN _____

MAD LIBS®
A GHASTLY GHOST STORY
(PART 2)

"Relax," said the _____. "You're _____ like a leaf,
NOUN   VERB ENDING IN "ING"

but you need not be afraid. I am a friendly _____." "Really?"
        NOUN

I said. "Wow! I can't wait for you to meet my _____."
      PLURAL NOUN

"I would love to, but unfortunately I can only reveal myself to the

first _____ who falls asleep," the ghost replied. And in the
  NOUN

blink of a/an _____, the ghost was gone. I ran to awaken
   PART OF THE BODY

my sleeping _____ to tell them what had happened,
    PLURAL NOUN

but they said they didn't believe me. They told me I'd lost all my

_____! But I could tell they wished they had seen the
PLURAL NOUN

_____ ghost. Sure enough, the next time I had a sleepover
ADJECTIVE

at my _____ house, each girl tried _____ to be
  ADJECTIVE   ADVERB

the first _____ to fall asleep and meet the friendly
    NOUN

_____!
NOUN

MAD LIBS® is fun to play with friends, but you can also play it by yourself! To begin with, DO NOT look at the story on the page below. Fill in the blanks on this page with the words called for. Then, using the words you have selected, fill in the blank spaces in the story.

Now you've created your own hilarious MAD LIBS® game!

HOT FUDGE SUNDAES

NOUN _____

NUMBER _____

PLURAL NOUN _____

ADJECTIVE _____

ADJECTIVE _____

ADJECTIVE _____

NOUN _____

NUMBER _____

PLURAL NOUN _____

NOUN _____

NOUN _____

NOUN _____

VERB (PAST TENSE) _____

PLURAL NOUN _____

ADJECTIVE _____

VERB _____

MAD LIBS®

HOT FUDGE SUNDAES

Making a hot fudge _____ is as simple as one, two,

NOUN

_____. All you need are the following _____:

NUMBER   PLURAL NOUN

 A pint of _____ ice cream

       ADJECTIVE

 1 jar of _____ fudge sauce

      ADJECTIVE

 1 cup of _____ nuts

      ADJECTIVE

 1 can of whipped _____

          NOUN

 _____ maraschino _____

   NUMBER   PLURAL NOUN

Scoop the ice _____ into a glass _____.

      NOUN   NOUN

Pour on a generous portion of hot _____ sauce, and

                NOUN

add a heaping mound of _____ cream. Sprinkle with

        VERB (PAST TENSE)

_____ and top off with a/an _____ cherry.

PLURAL NOUN   ADJECTIVE

Now _____ and enjoy!

   VERB

From SLEEPOVER PARTY MAD LIBS® • Copyright © 2008 by Penguin Random House LLC.

MAD LIBS® is fun to play with friends, but you can also play it by yourself! To begin with, DO NOT look at the story on the page below. Fill in the blanks on this page with the words called for. Then, using the words you have selected, fill in the blank spaces in the story.

Now you've created your own hilarious MAD LIBS® game!

TRUTH OR DARE (PART 1)

NOUN _____

PERSON IN ROOM (MALE) _____

NOUN _____

NUMBER _____

VERB (PAST TENSE) _____

NOUN _____

NUMBER _____

ADJECTIVE _____

VERB _____

NOUN _____

ADJECTIVE _____

NOUN _____

ADJECTIVE _____

TYPE OF LIQUID _____

NOUN _____

PLURAL NOUN _____

TYPE OF LIQUID _____

MAD LIBS®

TRUTH OR DARE (PART 1)

Let's play truth or dare! First, some truths:

Q: What is the name of the _____ you like?
NOUN

A: _____.
PERSON IN ROOM (MALE)

Q: What is one _____ no one knows about you?
NOUN

A: When I was _____ years old, I _____
NUMBER   VERB (PAST TENSE)

like a/an _____ in front of _____ people.
NOUN   NUMBER

Q: If you were stranded on a/an _____ island, what
ADJECTIVE

three things would you bring with you?

A: I couldn't _____ without my precious _____,
VERB   NOUN

my _____ _____, and a/an _____
ADJECTIVE   NOUN   ADJECTIVE

bottle of _____.
TYPE OF LIQUID

Q: What is the strangest _____ you have ever eaten?
NOUN

A: _____ dipped in _____.
PLURAL NOUN   TYPE OF LIQUID

MAD LIBS® is fun to play with friends, but you can also play it by yourself! To begin with, DO NOT look at the story on the page below. Fill in the blanks on this page with the words called for. Then, using the words you have selected, fill in the blank spaces in the story.

Now you've created your own hilarious MAD LIBS® game!

TRUTH OR DARE (PART 2)

ADJECTIVE _____

VERB _____

NOUN _____

ADJECTIVE _____

ADJECTIVE _____

NOUN _____

NOUN _____

VERB _____

PLURAL NOUN _____

ADJECTIVE _____

PART OF THE BODY (PLURAL) _____

NUMBER _____

MAD☺LIBS®

TRUTH OR DARE (PART 2)

And now for the dares!

DARE: Pretend you are a/an _____ puppy.
                                                    ADJECTIVE

_____ loudly and wag your _____.
        VERB   NOUN

DARE: Put on some _____ music and dance like
                              ADJECTIVE

a/an _____ _____ for one minute.
        ADJECTIVE   NOUN

DARE: Hop on one _____ while you _____
                            NOUN   VERB

and say the alphabet backward.

DARE: Take off your socks and _____ and step into
                                          PLURAL NOUN

the shower. Then turn on the _____ water and
                                          ADJECTIVE

yodel at the top of your _____ for _____
                              PART OF THE BODY (PLURAL)   NUMBER

seconds.

MAD LIBS® is fun to play with friends, but you can also play it by yourself! To begin with, DO NOT look at the story on the page below. Fill in the blanks on this page with the words called for. Then, using the words you have selected, fill in the blank spaces in the story.

Now you've created your own hilarious MAD LIBS® game!

A BAD NIGHTMARE

PERSON IN ROOM (FEMALE) _____

ADJECTIVE _____

PLURAL NOUN _____

NOUN _____

PLURAL NOUN _____

PLURAL NOUN _____

ADVERB _____

PART OF THE BODY (PLURAL) _____

NOUN _____

NOUN _____

SAME NOUN _____

VERB ENDING IN "ING" _____

VERB ENDING IN "ING" _____

MAD LIBS®

A BAD NIGHTMARE

One night when I slept over at my friend _____'s
PERSON IN ROOM (FEMALE)

house I had a/an _____ nightmare that scared the living
ADJECTIVE

_____ out of me. I dreamed I was in school, standing
PLURAL NOUN

in front of my English _____, giving a report on
NOUN

Shakespeare's _____, when I realized I wasn't wearing any
PLURAL NOUN

_____. Embarrassed beyond belief, I _____
PLURAL NOUN ADVERB

put my hands over my _____ and ran out of the
PART OF THE BODY (PLURAL)

classroom at breakneck _____. Suddenly, I was being
NOUN

chased by a wild _____! Just as the _____
NOUN SAME NOUN

was about to catch me, I woke up _____ with fright. I
VERB ENDING IN "ING"

spent the rest of the night _____ with the light on!
VERB ENDING IN "ING"

MAD LIBS® is fun to play with friends, but you can also play it by yourself! To begin with, DO NOT look at the story on the page below. Fill in the blanks on this page with the words called for. Then, using the words you have selected, fill in the blank spaces in the story.

Now you've created your own hilarious MAD LIBS® game!

MAKEOVER MADNESS

ADJECTIVE _____

PERSON IN ROOM (FEMALE) _____

PERSON IN ROOM (FEMALE) _____

ADJECTIVE _____

EXCLAMATION _____

NOUN _____

PART OF THE BODY _____

PART OF THE BODY _____

ADJECTIVE _____

PLURAL NOUN _____

NOUN _____

COLOR _____

NOUN _____

PLURAL NOUN _____

ADJECTIVE _____

VERB _____

ADVERB _____

PLURAL NOUN _____

NOUN _____

PART OF THE BODY (PLURAL) _____

MAD LIBS®
MAKEOVER MADNESS

A/An _____ scene to be played by _____
ADJECTIVE   PERSON IN ROOM (FEMALE)

and _____.
PERSON IN ROOM (FEMALE)

GIRL 1: I'm going to give you a/an _____ makeover.
ADJECTIVE

GIRL 2: _____! Will I look like a new _____?
EXCLAMATION   NOUN

GIRL 1: Yes, from head to _____. First, we'll brush your
PART OF THE BODY

_____ to make it sleek and _____.
PART OF THE BODY   ADJECTIVE

GIRL 2: What about my _____? My friends say my eyes
PLURAL NOUN

are my best _____.
NOUN

GIRL 1: They are. Applying _____ eye _____
COLOR   NOUN

will definitely bring out the color of your _____. And
PLURAL NOUN

changing your _____ clothes will also help.
ADJECTIVE

GIRL 2: You don't like the way I _____?
VERB

GIRL 1: You should try and dress more _____. Those
ADVERB

_____ you've been wearing are so last year. Trust me,
PLURAL NOUN

when we're finished, you'll be the talk of the _____.
NOUN

GIRL 2: I've got my _____ crossed!
PART OF THE BODY (PLURAL)

MAD LIBS® is fun to play with friends, but you can also play it by yourself! To begin with, DO NOT look at the story on the page below. Fill in the blanks on this page with the words called for. Then, using the words you have selected, fill in the blank spaces in the story.

Now you've created your own hilarious MAD LIBS® game!

HOW TO SING KARAOKE

ADJECTIVE _____

A PLACE _____

ADVERB _____

NOUN _____

ADJECTIVE _____

ADJECTIVE _____

ADJECTIVE _____

ADJECTIVE _____

ADJECTIVE _____

NOUN _____

ADVERB _____

PLURAL NOUN _____

NOUN _____

MAD LIBS®
HOW TO SING KARAOKE

Karaoke is a/an _____ form of entertainment that first
                        ADJECTIVE

became popular in (the) _____ and _____
                            A PLACE   ADVERB

caught on all over the _____. In karaoke, you sing
                            NOUN

along to a/an _____ song using a/an _____
                  ADJECTIVE   ADJECTIVE

microphone. You don't have to be a particularly good singer to sing

karaoke—you can even be a/an _____ singer. The most
                                    ADJECTIVE

important thing is to have a/an _____ time. Karaoke is
                                      ADJECTIVE

especially _____ at a sleepover party. You don't even
                ADJECTIVE

need a/an _____ machine! You can just turn up the
                NOUN

radio and sing _____. Just be sure to give other
                    ADVERB

_____ a turn—you don't want to be a/an
    PLURAL NOUN

_____ hog!
    NOUN

MAD LIBS® is fun to play with friends, but you can also play it by yourself! To begin with, DO NOT look at the story on the page below. Fill in the blanks on this page with the words called for. Then, using the words you have selected, fill in the blank spaces in the story.

Now you've created your own hilarious MAD LIBS® game!

SLEEPOVER, SCHMEEPOVER

ADJECTIVE _____

PLURAL NOUN _____

NUMBER _____

NOUN _____

NUMBER _____

NOUN _____

NOUN _____

PLURAL NOUN _____

NOUN _____

PLURAL NOUN _____

PLURAL NOUN _____

NOUN _____

PLURAL NOUN _____

ADJECTIVE _____

NOUN _____

The _____ thing about sleepover parties is that,
      ADJECTIVE

even though you're supposed to "sleep over," chances are you and

your _____ will catch fewer than _____ winks!
   PLURAL NOUN   NUMBER

It's always the same—you promise your mom and _____
                                              NOUN

that you'll go to bed before _____ o'clock, but instead
                             NUMBER

you stay up until the crack of _____. The next thing
                               NOUN

you know, you're waking up to the smell of fried _____
                                              NOUN

and scrambled _____ emanating from the
                              PLURAL NOUN

_____. After breakfast, you change out of your
              NOUN

_____, pack your _____, and stumble
   PLURAL NOUN   PLURAL NOUN

into your parents' _____ when they come to pick
                         NOUN

you up. If you're like most _____ your age, you'll
                          PLURAL NOUN

be so tired, you'll want to take a/an _____ nap
                                   ADJECTIVE

the minute you get home. Which gets a/an _____
                                        NOUN

thinking—maybe they should call them awake-overs instead!